WHISTLER

WHISTLER

Maria Costantino

Grange BOOKS

Published by Grange Books
An imprint of Grange Books PLC
The Grange
Grange Yard
London SE1 3AG

Produced by Saturn Books Ltd
Kiln House
210 New Kings Road
London SW6 4NZ

ISBN 1 85627 958 8

Printed in Singapore

PAGE 1: *Self-portrait* 1859:
see page 33.

PAGE 2: *The Little White Girl*:
see page 49.

BELOW: *The Blue Wave*: see
page 44.

CONTENTS

INTRODUCTION

Wit, aesthete, cosmopolitan, and dandy, James MacNeill Whistler, one of the outstanding artistic figures of the late 19th century, was both adored and hated by the social and artistic worlds in which he moved.

Whistler was born at Lowell, Massachusetts, on July 19, 1834, and by his early youth had already experienced an extraordinary cosmopolitan life. As a boy he had lived in St. Petersburg, Russia, where his civil engineer father was employed by the czar on a railroad construction project, and in 1848 he spent a short period at school in England. It was his family's intention that Whistler should have a military career, and he was enrolled at the leading United States military academy, at West Point. Despite his later dandy lifestyle, Whistler remained immensely proud of his military schooling even though he was discharged from West Point in 1854 for failing in chemistry classes!

By this time Whistler's interest in art had developed and he had already made a number of drawings and caricatures of his fellow students based on those by Honoré Daumier and Paul Gavarni. Following his dismissal from West Point, Whistler stayed in Baltimore with his mother, and while there he began his experiments with lithography. A brief spell in the United States Coast Geodetic Survey, where his principal role was to produce maps and topographical plans, gave Whistler a thorough understanding of etching techniques that would form the basis of his later artistic development.

Whistler's artistic career properly began in November 1855 with his arrival in Paris with an allowance of $350 per year and his desire to live "*la vie de Bohemie*" in the Latin Quarter. Although there was a growing number of Americans who were looking for artistic training in the Paris ateliers, Whistler had one major advantage over many of his fellow countrymen in so far as he was fairly fluent in French. In true Bohemian fashion, Whistler lived with a young milliner named Eloise, known as "La Tigresse" because of her temper, who also served as Whistler's model for a number of etchings.

It was as a graphic artist rather than as a painter that Whistler began his career. By the time he arrived in Paris there had been a great revival of interest in printmaking and new print departments had been opened in the galleries of the Musée du Luxembourg that contained prints by Delacroix, Gavarni, and Daubigny among others.

Whistler's painting training began when in 1856 he entered the atelier of Charles Gleyre and his circle of friends grew to include the novelist George du Maurier, L. M. Lamont (who became the model for the character "the Laird" in Maurier's novel *Trilby*), Joseph Rowley (who also appears in *Trilby* as "Taffy"), Alecco Ionides ("the Greek" in the same book), Henri Martin, and Edward Poynter. Du Maurier later introduced Whistler himself into his novel as Joe Sibley, the "idle apprentice," which reflected a characteristic view of Whistler although it was a misinterpretation of his temperament. In fact Whistler studied hard and followed his fellow students in the

RIGHT: Page 10 of Whistler's St Petersburg sketchbook, pencil and black ink, 14⅛ x 40⁷⁄₁₀ in.

BELOW LEFT: Academy Song of the Graduates, designed by Whistler at West Point, 1852.

BELOW: Page 11 of Whistler's St Petersburg sketchbook, pencil and black ink, 14⅛ x 40⁷⁄₁₀ in.

usual practice of copying old master paintings in the Louvre, where his choices included Boucher, Ingres, Veronese, and, most important, Velasquez.

Whistler's arrival in France had also coincided with a vogue for all things Spanish. Hispagnolisme had already been apparent in the work of French 18th-century painters like Fragonard and de Troy, and the taste had been widened by the Romantics like Hugo and Gautier. The marriage of Louis Napoleon to a Spanish beauty gave further impetus to the fashion, and Spanish painting gave a new excitement to the radical artists of France. For Whistler it was Velasquez's low tonalities, neutral colored backgrounds used to set off the figure or figures, that became his artistic aim.

At this early stage however, Whistler was primarily a Realist and his talents were most effectively demonstrated in his etchings rather than his paintings. His first set of etchings, *Twelve Etchings from Nature* (generally but erroneously termed the *French Set*), was the outcome of an August 1858 walking tour of northern France, Luxembourg, and the Rhineland that Whistler made with his artist friend Ernest Delaunoy. Whistler's "blossoming" as a painter really occurred after this when he came into contact with the circle of Realist painters.

In October 1858 Whistler met Henri Fantin-Latour in the Louvre where they were both copying the same picture. Latour took Whistler to the Café Molière, the meeting place of a circle of friends that included Alphonse Legros, Carolus-Duran, and Zacharie Astruc. There, according to the legend, Whistler showed his *French Set*. His entry proper to the Realist circle was sealed when Latour introduced Whistler to the "leader" of the Realists, Gustav Courbet.

In November 1858 Whistler left Paris for London, where he began his first important painting, a scene in the London home of his half sister Deborah Delano and her husband, Seymour Haden. *At The Piano* displays the considerable influence of Whistler's study of Dutch interiors as well as a resemblance to Fantin-Latour's *The Artist's Sisters Embroidering* (City Art Museum, St. Louis) and Degas's *Portrait of the Bellelei Family* (Louvre, Paris), both of which date from 1859, the year Whistler's own painting was completed.

In April Whistler sent this painting and two etchings to the Paris Salon. The official Salon was still the most prestigious place in which to have works shown and it was the goal of every artist in Paris to have their work accepted for exhibition. Although the etchings were accepted, *At The Piano* was refused. The painting depicts Deborah Delano at the piano watched by her 10-year-old daughter Annie. Both are wearing mourning for Whistler's father, Major George

ABOVE: Whistler met Carolus-Duran (seen here in later life with honours from the Academy) at the Café Molière.

RIGHT: *Fumette*, an 1859 etching of Whistler's mistress.

Washington Whistler, who died in 1849. Annie's short white dress was deemed the appropriate style and color of mourning for Victorian children.

Although it was rejected at the 1859 Salon, Whistler was able to exhibit *At The Piano* in the studio of François Bonvin, where it was seen and admired by Gustav Courbet and the Realists. Almost immediately Whistler was firmly placed in the ranks of the most avant garde French painters. The following year *At The Piano* was shown in London at the Royal Academy, where it was admired by the members of the Pre-Raphaelite Brotherhood — Millais, Hunt, and Rossetti. It was not until 1867 that the painting was finally accepted at the Paris Salon. But even before this it was evident that many artists in Paris were aware of Whistler's composition and experiments in tonal harmonies: Both Degas and Manet also produced portraits of women at the piano.

The friendly reception that *At The Piano* received at the Royal Academy no doubt contributed to Whistler's

Imp.Delatre. Rue S.t Jacques. 171.

decision to spend more time in London. In May 1859 he left Paris to live with the Hadens on Sloane Street. A true Realist, Whistler found his themes in the world around him and he made a series of etchings based on scenes around Greenwich Park and the River Thames. He later took lodgings in Wapping, in the London docklands, and began the *Thames Set* etchings. Whistler was by no means the first, nor would he be the last artist to be fascinated by the river: Canaletto, Constable, Turner, Monet, Derrain, and de Stael were all captivated by the river's movement and qualities of light. Yet Whistler's painted views of the Thames from the 1860s parallel developments in his figure compositions away from Realism toward Idealism.

At the beginning of the decade Whistler began by painting *Wapping* and *The Thames in Ice*, both of which depict the reality of the industrialized river. By the end of the decade, following a visit to Trouville in 1865 and the influence of Japanese art, Whistler's views of the Thames, such as *Battersea Reach from*

Lindsey House (1864-71) and *Grey and Silver: Chelsea Wharf* (1864-8), demonstrate his move away from the Realist dark-toned impasto style of painting toward a freer handling of paint and a lighter palette.

As in Paris, in London Whistler formed an attachment, this time with the red-haired Irish girl Joanna Hiffernan. Jo had first posed for Whistler in Paris in 1861 for *Symphony in White No.1: The White Girl*. In this full-length, life-size portrait, Jo is posed in a shallow space against the background of a white curtain. Instead of the fashionable Victorian crinoline, Jo wears a simple unconstructed dress not unlike the gowns favored by the Pre-Raphaelite models Elizabeth Siddal and Janie Morris. The association with the Pre-Raphaelite Brotherhood is further strengthened by the white lily that Jo holds in her left hand. The only notes of color are to be found in Jo's loosened hair falling over her shoulders and in the flower-patterned carpet. Rejected by the Royal Academy exhibition in 1862, this painting was sent by Whistler to Paris, where the following year it was one

BELOW: *At the Piano* was shown in London at the Royal Academy, where it was admired by the members of the Pre-Raphaelite Brotherhood. See page 34/5.

RIGHT: *Weary (Jo Resting)*, 1863. Drypoint on Japanese paper.

ABOVE: Self-portrait, *Artist in his studio*, painted in oil on cardboard.

RIGHT: Beatrix Whistler.

of 4,000 other works rejected by the Salon. In response to the growing chorus of criticism directed against the Salon and its jury system, the emperor set up the now famous Salon des Refusés, and *The White Girl* was hung in the Palais d'Industrie alongside paintings by Cézanne, Pissarro, and Monet.

The White Girl was variously interpreted by Victorian audiences as the depiction of a young woman on the morning following her bridal night, a portrait of a psychic medium (the 1860s saw a craze for spiritualism), and a "fallen woman." But one of the most popular readings of the painting at the time was

LEFT: *The Blue Dress* (Study for Mrs Frances Leyland), pastel, 1871.

RIGHT: *Nocturne: Battersea Bridge*, pastel, 1872.

BELOW: The 1870s saw Whistler at work on portraits in which he sought to make an "arrangement" of forms and color and to impart information about the character of each sitter. The finest example is *Arrangement in Grey and Black: Portrait of the Painter's Mother* (1871).

LEFT: *Maud Franklin*, pastel, 1878.

RIGHT: *Little Venice*, an etching (7⁵⁄₁₆ x 10 ⁷⁄₁₆ in.) of 1879. The Metropolitan Museum of Art Harris Brisbane Dick Fund, 1917. (17.3.85)

provided by Wilkie Collins's novels *Woman in White* (which parallels Whistler's figure) and *The Moonstone*, the plot of which revolves around the theme of hypnosis and sleepwalking. For Whistler, however, *The White Girl* had no subject but that of a model posing in the studio!

Jo was to model for some of Whistler's most famous works, including *Wapping* (1860-4) and *Symphony in White No.3* (1865-7); she remained his mistress until sometime in the late 1860s or early 1870s, when she was "replaced" by Maud Franklin, the model for *Arrangement in Yellow* and *Grey: Effie Deans* (1876-8). Effie Deans was a character in Sir Walter Scott's novel *The Heart of Mid-Lothian* (1818)

who is falsely accused of murdering her illegitimate baby; Maud would also be the model for *Note in Red: The Siesta* (1883-4) as well as a number of watercolors. Their relationship would later end, and in 1888 Whistler married Beatrice, the widow of architect E. W. Goodwin

The precise date of Whistler's introduction to oriental art is by no means certain, but it most likely occurred in the 1850s in Paris, when Félix Braquemond showed Hiroshige's volume of woodcuts, the *Manga,* to a group of artists that included besides Whistler, Degas, Manet, and Fantin-Latour. All became passionate about Japanese art which would also arouse a great deal of enthusiasm

in England. Initially, Whistler's use of oriental elements in his pictures was marked by something of a "fancy-dress" spirit. His earliest "oriental" picture — *Rose and Silver: La Princesse du Pays de la Porcelaine* (1863-4) — is the portrait of Christina Spartall, the daughter of the Greek Consul-General in London. While Christina wears a kimono and her pose is derived from that found in a Japanese print, overall the painting bears no relation to the radical designs found in Japanese art.

It was only with *Caprice in Purple and Gold: The Golden Screen* (1864) that Whistler began to simplify the construction of the painting and impose on it a rhythmic and decorative unity. Yet even with a profound taste for the exotic, Whistler could not forget the local scene. In *Variations in Flesh Colour and Green: The Balcony* (1864-5) Whistler combined the scene with a background composed of the Thames with its factories and smoking chimneys!

By the late 1860s Whistler had assimilated the Japanese principles of simplicity of design and economy of expression into his own art. His growing understanding of Japanese art and design and his friendships with British architects like Godwin and Jeckyll, finally culminated in his uniting art and architecture in the decorative masterpiece *The Peacock Room* (1876). Yet it is only in certain of his watercolor landscapes of the 1870s that Whistler dispensed with illusionistic representation in favor of treating pictorial space as a flat field on which to arrange near-abstract forms.

The mid-1860s were particularly decisive years in Whistler's career. Although he was discovering new ways of handling paint and pictorial space, he believed that he had failed to paint his Realist masterpiece on the subject of the artist in his studio. Whistler had hoped that this ambitious project — a composition measuring 10 feet by 6 feet — would rival Fantin-Latour's *Homage to Delacroix*, but his inability to complete the work seems to have contributed to his growing awareness that his painting techniques and training, received in Gleyre's studio, were inadequate. This awareness would, in 1867, lead Whistler to reject bitterly Courbet and the Realists as well as lose him many of his former friends. Furthermore, it encouraged his impetuous flight to Valparaiso to fight alongside the Chileans in their struggle for independence from Spain. Whistler, however, was to take no part in the actual fighting: When the Spanish bombarded the defenseless Valparaiso on March 31 he fled the town on horseback.

Soon after, hostilities ceased and Whistler stayed on for a while in Valparaiso and then in Santiago before setting sail for England in September 1866. A

number of seascapes date from this period, including *Nocturne: The Solent* (1886), which represents the first hints of the nocturnes of the 1870s with its blue-tone twilight atmosphere; *Crepscule In Flesh Colour and Green: Valparaiso* (1866), where the treatment of the sky still acknowledges the debt to Courbet but nevertheless shows a move toward a more unified surface treatment; and *Nocturne In Blue and Gold: Valparaiso Bay* (1866), Whistler's first attempt at a night scene, where no attempt has been made to present recessional perspective and where dabs of paint indicate the presence of lights, a technique he would exploit more fully in *Nocturne In Black and Gold: The Falling Rocket* (1875).

Early in the 1860s Whistler had complained to Fantin-Latour about the difficulties of capturing the effects of light and weather when working "en plein air." Part of the problem was to do with the painting techniques he had learned in Paris, which were adequate for working in the studio but far more difficult to use when working out of doors. The problem was finally resolved in the *Nocturne* paintings of the 1870s, when Whistler simply worked indoors

ABOVE: *The Palaces*, an etching (9¹⁵⁄₁₆ x 14 in.) of 1879. The Metropolitan Museum of Art. Gift of Felix M. Warburg and his Family, 1941. (41.1.196)

RIGHT: *A Symphony* – a caricature of Whistler by Leslie Ward, the artist 'Spy', which appeared in *Vanity Fair* on 12 January 1878.

painting views of the Thames from balconies or through windows! When he did venture out on to the river he chose quiet times — at times of extreme cold as in *Chelsea in Ice*, in the fog, and finally, when the river "slept" at night. Yet there still remained the problem of how to capture in the studio what he had seen outside. The key to the solution was Whistler's memory: He began to develop a mnemonic system as a means of creating a mental picture while he was outside that could be translated on to the canvas once he was back inside the studio. The "translation" had to be done as quickly as possible — and Whistler turned his attention to the techniques of the English watercolorists.

To paint the *Nocturne* series, Whistler invented a medium of his own which he called his "sauce." The "sauce" was a liquid mixture of copal (a kind of resin), turpentine, and linseed oil. On his prepared canvases

or panels Whistler applied a gray or red ground over which he washed his liquid colors, lightening or darkening the tones as he worked. In order to stop the "sauce" from running off the canvases, they had to be painted flat on the floor. Although the mixture would later prove somewhat unstable and many paintings would suffer greatly from deterioration, the medium allowed Whistler to work very quickly, often capturing the desired effects in just over an hour. More often than not, however, he would abandon the canavses in which he failed. The finished pictures were finally laid out to dry in the garden.

The designation "nocturne" in fact was not Whistler's but one given to the paintings by Frederick Leyland. The first was *Nocturne: Blue and Silver — Chelsea* (1871), and for a period Whistler confined his subject matter to a stretch of the Thames between the Westminster and Battersea bridges. The series (if it can really be called that) includes *Nocturne: Grey and Silver* (1873-5), one of Whistler's most simplified nocturnes, which consists of three bands of gray-black and deep blue, and two of his most controversial paintings, *Nocturne: Blue and Gold — Old Battersea Bridge* (1872-7) and *Nocturne in Black and Gold: The Falling Rocket* (1875). Whistler's atmospheric evocation of fireworks falling over Cremorna gardens led the critic John Ruskin to attack Whistler in print with the words: "I have seen and heard much of Cockney impudence before now; but never expected to hear a cocomb ask two hundred guineas for flinging a pot of paint in the public's face." Over this sentence Whistler sued Ruskin for libel. During the trial in 1878 Whistler tried to avoid referring to his painting as "pictures." Instead he called them "arrangements," "symphonies," or "moonlight effects." The outcome of the trial: Ruskin lost and Whistler was awarded damages of a farthing — a quarter of one penny — but not his court costs. While Whistler was at least vindicated in the courtroom, the British public and many of Britain's leading artists continued to be incensed by his paintings. When *Old Battersea Bridge* — which was one of the paintings produced as "evidence" during the trial — was offered for sale as late as 1886, the assembled audience at Christie's sale room showed their disapproval by hissing!

In an apparently conscious continuation of his argument with Ruskin over the issue of realism in art, in 1880 Whistler painted *Nocturne: Blue and Gold — St Mark's, Venice*. Whistler was in Venice at the same time as the painter John Whatton Bunney, who, at Ruskin's request, was painting a huge, stone-by-stone visual record of the west front of the basilica. Bunney's view and Whistler's are almost the same except that Bunney's painting shows St. Mark's in daylight. It is significant that Whistler chose to include the scaffolding erected for the restoration works on the building — restorations to which Ruskin was violently opposed. Somehow Bunney, in his pursuit of "visual truth" managed to leave out the scaffolding from his composition — even though it took six years for him to complete his painting and it would have been difficult to overlook its presence!

In addition to the *Nocturne* works, the 1870s saw Whistler at work on a number of portraits. In each he sought to make an "arrangement" of forms and color and to impart information about the character of each sitter. The finest example is, of course, *Arrangement in Grey and Black: Portrait of the Painter's Mother* (1871), where the simple beauty of the composition and color is balanced by the sense of the widow's character. The seated pose adopted by Anna Matilda MacNeill in fact had a number of historical precedents: the statue of Agrippina in the Capitol, Canova's portrait of *La Mère* (Napoleon's mother) at Chatsworth House in Derbyshire, and even Rembrandt's painting *Bathsheba*. Originally Anna was posed standing (X-rays of the painting have revealed the original position) and a variety of techniques were used from thick impasto to the scraping away of paint to reveal the canvas and create highlights. For years Whistler reworked the painting; unfortunately his mother did not live to see it completed.

Other commissioned portraits of the 1870s include *Arrangement in Grey and Black No.2: Portrait of Thomas Carlyle* (1872-3), a portrait of the great Victorian historian and social critic; *Harmony in Grey and Green: Miss Cicely Alexander* (1872-74), the eight-year-old daughter of a banker who was required to pose for over 70 sessions, each lasting several hours; *Arrangement in Black No.2: Portrait of Mrs. Louis Huth* (1872-73); and *Arrangement in Black No.3: Sir Henry Irving as Philip II of Spain* (1876), a portrait of the great Victorian actor who at the time of this portrait was appearing in Tennyson's verse play *Queen Mary Tudor*.

In 1876 Whistler received a commission from Frederick R. Leyland, a model of Victorian enterprise. Born into a poor Liverpool family Leyland had been an apprentice in a shipping company until he bought the company in 1873. Self-educated, Leyland sought to cast off his origins and his "nouveau riche" tag by amassing a collection of Renaissance and contemporary artworks. In 1876 Leyland had bought a house at Prince's Gate in London and had commissioned Thomas Jeckyll to adapt the living room to house his collection of oriental porcelain and Whistler to undertake a decorative scheme to compliment his painting *La Princesse du Pays de la Porcelaine*, which hung at one end of the room.

ABOVE: Five studies in
drypoint by Mortimer
Mempes of Whistler.

Whistler reworked a peacock scheme that he had originally suggested for another patron, W.C.Alexander, but which had been rejected as too expensive.

The walls and ceiling Whistler decorated with peacock-feather drawings — the ceiling paintings were achieved by fastening the paintbrush to a fishing rod. They were completed by October 1876. At this stage Whistler asked for his fee of 2,000 guineas, but Leyland refused to pay more than 1,000, claiming that the artist had exceeded in the terms of the commission. Nevertheless Whistler continued with the decorations and early in 1877 held a press view of the room, at which time he distributed a pamphlet, *Harmony in Blue and Gold: The Peacock Room.* Leyland, however, seemed to be under the impression that the gathering was to be of invited fellow artists, friends, and patrons and not members of the press and public. This was the last straw, and patron and painter argued furiously over costs and publicity. Finally Leyland deliberately insulted Whistler by paying his fee in pounds (like an ordinary tradesman) instead of the guineas acceptable to a gentleman. It is possible that Whistler never saw the Peacock Room again, as he was barred from ever entering the Leyland house. In 1904 the entire room was bought by C.L.Freer, dismantled, shipped, and reerected in Detroit. It eventually found its final resting place in the

ABOVE LEFT: *Behind the Arsenal*: see page 86.

LEFT: *The Ocean Wave*, watercolor on paper, 5 x 6¹⁵⁄₁₆ in. Painted c. 1883.

ABOVE: *The Peacock Room*: see page 74.

Freer Gallery of Art in Washington.

Following the publicity of the Ruskin trial, the debts incurred to pay for his court costs, coupled with his own extravagance and the very public row with Leyland, Whistler in the end was forced into bankruptcy in May 1879. In place of the "high society" patrons of portraits in the 1870s, there now came sitters from the "demi-monde," like Valerie Meux — *Arrangement in Black No.5: Lady Meux* (1881) — who despite "marrying-up" and her claims to be a legitimate actress was in fact better known to many as Val Reece, who worked at the Casino de Venise in Holborn, a dance hall that was a regular haunt of prostitutes. Other sitters included the actress Lily Langtry and the scandalous divorcée Lady Colin Campbell. (Both their portraits were unfortunately destroyed.)

Other clients with higher social credentials tended to be Americans or Whistler's "close friends and

admirers," such as Theodore Duret in *Arrangement in Flesh Colour and Black* (1883-84) — he was an art critic and collector of works by Degas, Monet, and the Impressionists — and the mother-in-law of the American painter Mary Cassatt in *Arrangement in Black No 8: Portrait of Mrs. Cassatt.*

Yet precisely because so many of his sitters in the 1880s were not like his earlier conservative clientele, Whistler now had much greater freedom to experiment with costumes, poses, and gestures; to explore the contrasts between black and white; and to further his investigations into tonal painting.

Despite the setbacks of the previous decade, by the 1880s Whistler had nonetheless earned an international reputation and his work was on show in Austria, France, Germany, and the United States, as well as in Britain. But in the last years of his life he was to devote much of his time to graphic works, producing more than 200 prints, of which the majority

Ernest Haskell's portrait of
Whistler of 1898; a litho-
graphic reproduction of a
drawing.

Self-portrait, 1859.
Drypoint, 8⅞ x 6 in.

Aubrey Beardsley's caricature of Whistler. Pen and
ink (8⁵⁄₁₆ x 4⁵⁄₈).

By the Balcony; lithograph on
paper, 8½ x 5½ in. Produced
1896.

were etchings of "impressions" of London and Paris street life. Celebrated once more, Whistler was again in demand as a portrait painter: the Duke of Marlborough commissioned him, but he unfortunately died and prevented the painting's completion, and in 1851 Whistler painted the portrait of the most elegant and outrageous dandy of the time — and the reputed model for Des Esseintes in Huysman's novel *A Rebours — Arrangement in Black and Gold: Comte Robert de Montesquieu.*

Wealthy American collectors were also seeking him out, such as Isabella Stewart Gardner and George Vanderbilt, whose portrait Whistler painted from 1897-1903. Yet he was having difficulty in finishing these commissioned portraits to his own satisfaction, and consequently few of his sitters received their portraits before Whistler's death in 1903.

Despite the increasingly apparent problem of the deterioration of many of the paintings produced in the 1870s and 1880s, Whistler continued to experiment with new painting techniques and to rework his paintings until he was completely satisfied. In his final years and following the death of his wife, Beatrice, in 1896, Whistler developed an interest (some of his unkinder critics would say an unhealthy interest) in painting young girls. Some studies show the continued influence of Velasquez, others the "sfumato" style of the Symbolist painter Eugène Carrier. In addition to these studies Whistler continued to paint his small open-air sketches and his passion for water and river scenes did not diminish. The series of seascapes painted at Pourville in the summer of 1899 remain some of his most outstanding paintings. In some Whistler returned to the theme of the single figure on a beach, while in others, though the compositions were often small scale, his color became increasingly evocative.

One of the most striking paintings of his last years is *Gold and Brown: Self Portrait* (1896-98) the portrait he wished to be remembered by. Suitably for the president of the International Society of Sculptors, Painters and Gravers, the American-born, French-trained, and English-based artist wears a wry smile and the tiny red ribbon of the Legion d'Honneur, which he had been awarded in 1892.

LEFT: *Study*, lithograph on paper, 10¼ x 6½ in.

BELOW: *The Smithy*, etching and drypoint on paper, 6⅞ x 9 in. Produced 1880s.

The Cobbler c. 1850
Watercolor on paper, 4⅛ x 5⅞ in.
Freer Gallery of Art, Smithsonian, Washington, DC

The Kitchen c. 1850
Watercolor and pencil on paper, 12 x 7¾ in.
Freer Gallery of Art, Smithsonian, Washington, DC

The Kitchen 1858
Etching, 9¹⁵⁄₁₆ x 14 in.
S. P. Avery Collection, Miriam and Ira D. Wallach Division of Art, Prints and Photographs
The New York Public Library, Astor, Lenox and Tilden Foundations

Self-Portrait 1859

Etching.

S. P. Avery Collection, Miriam and Ira D. Wallach Division of Art, Prints and Photographs

The New York Public Library, Astor, Lenox and Tilden Foundations

At the Piano 1858-9
Oil on canvas, 26⅜ x 36⅟₁₆.
Bequest of Louise Taft Semple, The Taft Museum, Cincinnati, OH

The Thames in Ice 1860
Oil on canvas, 29⅜ x 21¾ in.
Freer Gallery of Art, Smithsonian, Washington, DC

Annie Haden 1860
Etching.
S. P. Avery Collection, Miriam and Ira D. Wallach Division of Art, Prints and Photographs
The New York Public Library, Astor, Lenox and Tilden Foundations

The Limeburner 1860
Etching.
S. P. Avery Collection, Miriam and Ira D. Wallach Division of Art, Prints and Photographs
The New York Public Library, Astor, Lenox and Tilden Foundations

The Miser 1861
Drypoint on paper, 4⅝ x 6¼ in.
Freer Gallery of Art, Smithsonian, Washington, DC

Wapping on Thames 1860-4
Oil on canvas, 28⅜ x 40⅛ in.
National Gallery of Art, Washington, DC
John Hay Whitney Collection

Coast of Brittany (or Alone with the Tide) 1861
Oil on canvas.
In memory of William Arnold Healy, given by his daughter, Susie Healy Camp.
Wadsworth Atheneum, Hartford, CT

Blue and Silver: The Blue Wave, Biarritz 1862
Oil on canvas.
Hillstead Museum, Farmington, CT

The White Girl: Symphony in White No. 1 1862
Oil on canvas, 84½ x 42½ in.
National Gallery of Art, Washington, DC
Harris Whittemore Collection

Variations in Flesh Colour and Green – The Balcony 1864-70
Oil on wood panel, 24¼ x 19¼ in.
Freer Gallery of Art, Smithsonian, Washington, DC

Caprice in Purple and Gold: The Golden Screen 1864
Oil on wood panel, 19⅝ x 27 in.
Freer Gallery of Art, Smithsonian, Washington, DC

The Little White Girl: Symphony in White No. 2 1864
Oil on canvas, 30⅛ x 20⅛ in.
The Tate Gallery, London

Harmony in Blue and Silver: Trouville 1865
Oil on canvas.
Isabella Stewart Gardner Museum, Boston, MA

Nocturne: Blue and Gold – Valparaiso 1866-74
Oil on canvas, 29¾ x 19¾ in.
Freer Gallery of Art, Smithsonian, Washington, DC

Fumette 1858
Etching
S. P. Avery Collection, Miriam and Ira D. Wallach Division of Art, Prints and Photographs
The New York Public Library, Astor, Lenox and Tilden Foundations

Crepuscule in Opal, Trouville 1867
Oil on canvas.
Toledo Museum of Art, Toledo, OH

Morning Glories 1865-70
Chalk and pastel on brown paper, 10¼ x 6⅜ in.
Freer Gallery of Art, Smithsonian, Washington, DC

Sailboats in Blue Water 1870-80
Watercolor on off-white paper, 8½ x 5 in.
Harvard University Art Museums, Cambridge, MA
Bequest of Grenville L. Winthrop

Annabel Lee c. 1870
Pastel on brown paper, 12¾ x 7⅟₁₆ in.
Freer Gallery of Art, Smithsonian, Washington, DC

Nocturne in Blue and Silver: Chelsea 1871
Oil on wood, 19¾ x 29¼ in.
The Tate Gallery, London

Salute: Sundown 1880
Pastel on color paper, 7⅗₀ x 10½ in.
© Hunterian Art Gallery, University of Glasgow

Arrangement in Gray: Portrait of the Painter 1872
Oil on canvas, 29 x 21 in.
Bequest of Henry Glover Stevens in memory of Ellen P.
Stevens and Mary M. Stevens
©The Detroit Institute of Arts

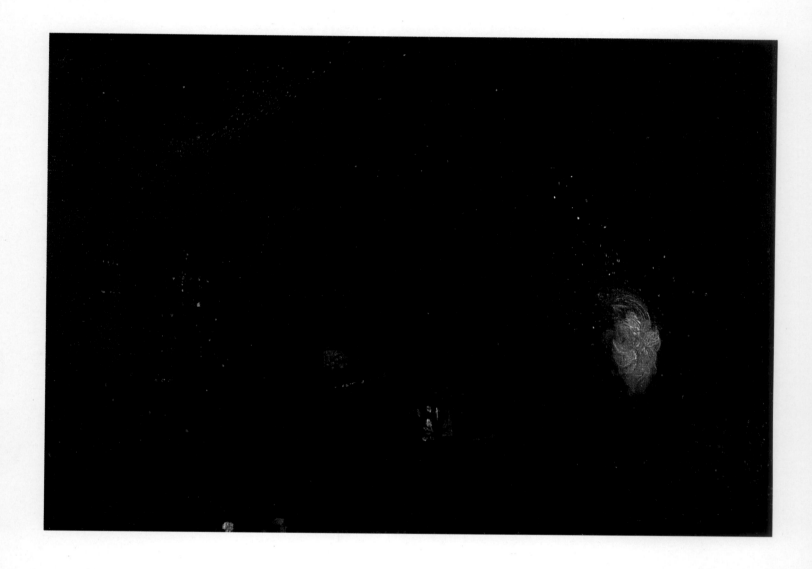

Nocturne in Black and Gold: The Firewheel 1872-7
Oil on canvas.
The Tate Gallery, London

Gold and Grey: The Sunny Shower, Dordrecht 1872
Watercolor, 5 x 8½ in.
© Hunterian Art Gallery, University of Glasgow

Nocturne in Blue and Silver: Cremorne Lights 1872
Oil on canvas, 19¾ x 29¼ in.
The Tate Gallery, London

Arrangement in Grey and Black No. 2: Thomas Carlyle 1872-3
Oil on canvas, 67⅓ x 56½ in.
Glasgow Museums: Art Gallery & Museum, Kelvingrove, Scotland

Harmony in Grey and Green: Miss Cicely Alexander 1872
Oil on canvas, 22 x 29⅛ in.
The Tate Gallery, London

Nocturne in Blue and Gold: Old Battersea Bridge c. 1872-5
Oil on canvas, 26¾ x 20 in.
The Tate Gallery, London

Symphony in Flesh Color and Pink: Portrait of Frances Leyland 1873
Oil on canvas.
© The Frick Collection, New York

Arrangement in Black: Portrait of F. R. Leyland 1870-3
Oil on canvas, 75⅞ x 36⅛ in.
Free Gallery of Art, Smithsonian, Washington, DC

Nocturne: Gray and Silver 1873
Oil on canvas.
John G. Johnson Collection, Philadelphia Museum of Art, PH

**Nocturne in Black and Gold, the Falling
Rocket** c. 1873
Oil on oak panel, 23⁷⁄₁₀ x 18⅔ in.
Gift of Dexter M. Ferry, Jr
©The Detroit Institute of Arts

Arrangement in White and Black c. 1873
Oil on canvas, 75⅜ x 35¾ in.
Freer Gallery of Art, Smithsonian, Washington, DC

Harmony in Blue and Gold: The Peacock Room 1876-7
Oil paint and metal leaf on canvas, 167⅞ x 398 in.
Freer Gallery of Art, Smithsonian, Washington, DC

Arrangement in Black and Brown: The Fur Jacket 1877
Oil on canvas, 76⅜ x 36½ in.
Worcester Art Museum, Worcester, MA
Museum purchase

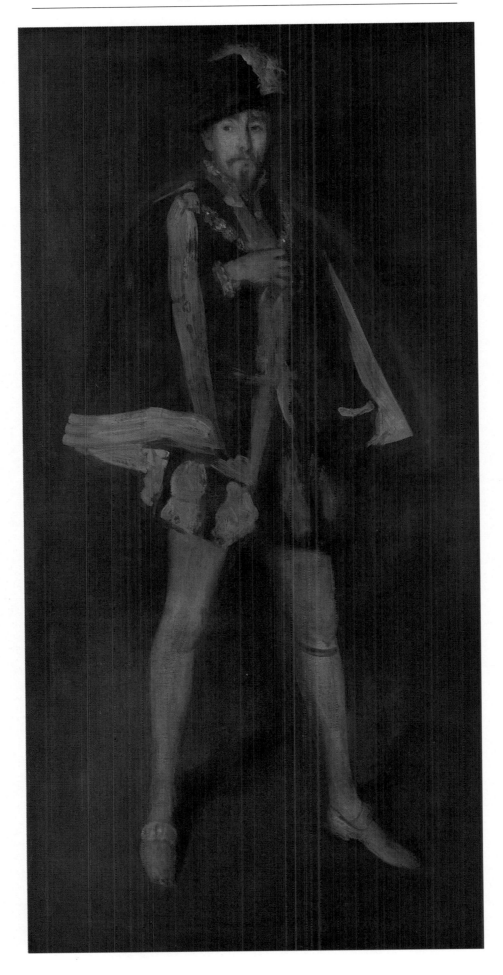

Arrangement in Black No. 3: Sir Henry Irving as Philip II of Spain 1877
Oil on canvas, 84¾ x 42¾ in.
The Metropolitan Museum of Art, Rogers Fund, 1910. (10.86)

Nocturne in Grey and Gold: Chelsea Snow 1876
Oil on canvas, 18¼ x 23¾ in.
Harvard University Art Museums, Cambridge, MA
Bequest of Grenville L. Winthrop

Nocturne: Grey and Silver – Chelsea Embankmemt
Oil on canvas, 24⅝ x 18⅝ in.
Freer Gallery of Art, Smithsonian, Washington, DC

The Lagoon, Venice: Nocturne in Blue and Silver 1879
Oil on canvas, 20 x 25¾ in.
Emily L. Ainsley Fund
Courtesy of Museum of Fine Arts, Boston, MA

Old Battersea Bridge 1879
Etching.
S. P. Avery Collection, Miriam and Ira D. Wallach Division of Art, Prints and Photographs
The New York Public Library, Astor, Lenox and Tilden Foundations

Note in Pink and Purple – The Studio Early 1880s
Watercolor on paper, 12 x 9 in.
Freer Gallery of Art, Smithsonian, Washington, DC

Millie Finch Early 1880s
Watercolor on paper, 11¾ x 8⅞ in.
Freer Gallery of Art, Smithsonian, Washington, DC

Nocturne: Silver and Opal – Chelsea Early 1880s
Oil on wood panel, 8 x 10⅛ in.
Freer Gallery of Art, Smithsonian, Washington, DC

Behind the Arsenal 1880
Pastel on brown paper, 9⁹⁄₁₀ x 6⁷⁄₁₀ in.
Harvard University Art Museums,Cambridge, MA
Bequest of Grenville L. Winthrop

The Mast 1880
Etching on paper, 13⅜ x 6⁷⁄₁₆ in.
Freer Gallery of Art, Smithsonian, Washington, DC

The Steps 1879-89
Crayon and pastel on grey paper, 7⅝ x 11⅞ in.
Freer Gallery of Art, Smithsonian, Washington, DC

Note in Flesh Color: The Guidecca c. 1880
Pastel on paper.
The Mead Art Museum, Amherst College, MA

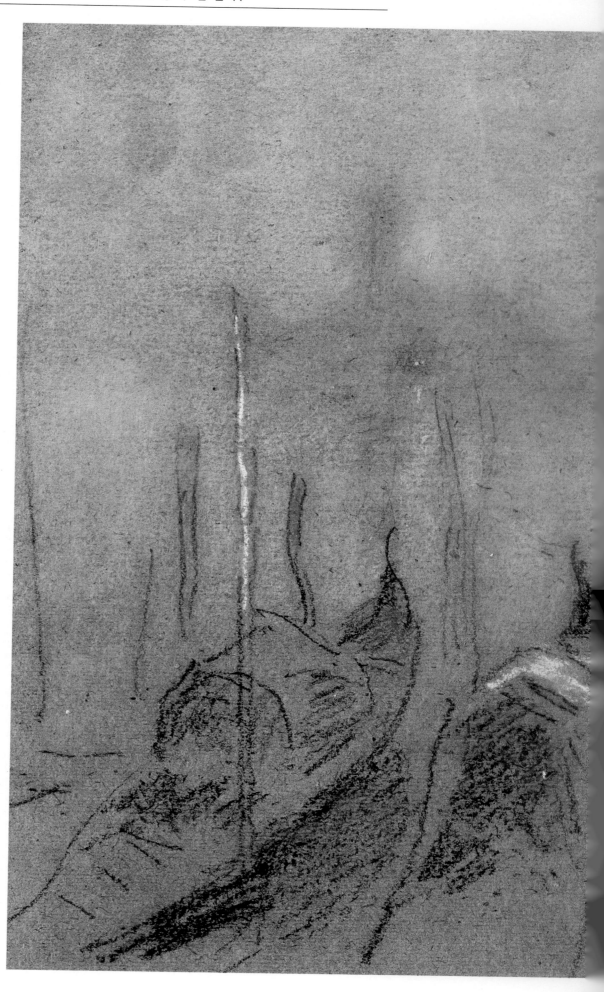

Nocturne: San Giorgio 1879-80
Chalk and pastel on grey paper, 8 x 11⅞ in.
Freer Gallery of Art, Smithsonian, Washington, DC

Valerie, Lady Meux 1881
Oil on canvas.
© The Frick Collection, New York

Arrangement in Flesh Colour and Black: Portrait of Théodore Duret 1883
Oil on canvas, 76⅛ x 35¾ in.
The Metropolitan Museum of Art, Wolfe Fund, Catherine Lorillard Wolfe Collection, 1913.
(13.20). Photograph by Paul Warchol.

Arrangement in Black: The Lady in the Yellow Buskin; Lady Archibald Campbell 1882-4
Oil on canvas, 86 x 43½ in.
Philadelphia Museum of Art
W. P. Wilstach Collection

The Beggars – Winter c. 1880
Chalk and pastel on brown paper, 11⅞ x 7¹⁵⁄₁₆ in.
Freer Gallery of Art, Smithsonian, Washington, DC

The Grand Canal, Venice c. 1879-80
Pastel on grey paper, 6⅞ x 10⅝ in.
Freer Gallery of Art, Smithsonian, Washington, DC

Green and Silver: Beaulieu, Touraine c. 1879-80
Pastel on grey paper, 5⅛ x 8½ in.
Freer Gallery of Art, Smithsonian, Washington, DC

The Little Note in Orange and Blue: The Sweet Shop 1884
Oil on canvas, 4¾ x 8¼ in.
Isabella Stewart Gardner Museum, Boston, MA

The Angry Sea 1884
Oil on wood panel, 4⅞ x 8½ in.
Freer Gallery of Art, Smithsonian, Washington, DC

Resting in Bed 1884
Watercolor on paper, 6¹¹⁄₁₆ x 9⁷⁄₁₆ in.
Freer Gallery of Art, Smithsonian, Washington, DC

Note in Blue and Opal: The Sun Cloud 1884
Oil on wood panel, 4⅞ x 8½ in.
Freer Gallery of Art, Smithsonian, Washington, DC

Pink Note: Shelling Peas Early 1880s
Watercolor on paper, 9⁹⁄₁₆ x 5¾ in.
Freer Gallery of Art, Smithsonian, Washington, DC

Chelsea Shops Early 1880s
Oil on wood panel, 5¼ x 9¼ in.
Freer Gallery of Art, Smithsonian, Washington, DC

Flower Market: Dieppe 1885
Watercolor on paper, 5¹⁄₁₆ x 8¼ in.
Freer Gallery of Art, Smithsonian, Washington, DC

Maud Reading in Bed 1887
Watercolor
The Walters Art Gallery, Baltimore, MD

Harmony in Red Lamplight 1884-6
Oil on canvas, 76⅒ x 35¾ in.
© Hunterian Art Gallery, University of Glasgow

Little Scheveningen: Gray Note 1890s
Watercolor, 4¾ x 8½ in.
Gift of Walter Gay
Courtesy of Museum of Fine Arts, Boston, MA

Rose and Silver: Portrait of Mrs. Whibley Early 1890s
Watercolor on paper, 11⅛ x 7⅜ in.
Freer Gallery of Art, Smithsonian, Washington, DC

Miss Lillian Woakes 1890-1
Oil on canvas, 21 x 14 in.
© The Phillips Collection, Washington, DC

Arrangement in Black and Gold: Comte Robert de Montesquiou-Fezenac 1891
Oil on canvas.
© The Frick Collection, New York

The Garden 1891
Lithograph on paper, 6¹¹⁄₁₆ x 7³⁄₁₆ in.
Freer Gallery of Art, Smithsonian, Washington, DC

The Arabian c. 1890-2
Pastel on colored paper, 7¹⁄₁₀ x 11 in.
© Hunterian Art Gallery, University of Glasgow

Nude Figure Reclining 1893
Etching on paper, 7½ x 10⁷⁄₁₆ in.
Freer Gallery of Art, Smithsonian, Washington, DC

Violet and Silver – The Deep Sea 1893
Oil on canvas, 19¾ x 28⅞in
Gift of Clara Margaret Lynch in memory of John A. Lynch, 1955.743
The Art Institute of Chicago, IL

The Pantheon, from the Terrace of the Luxembourg Gardens 1893
Lithograph on paper, 7⅛ x 6⁵⁄₁₆ in.
Freer Gallery of Art, Smithsonian, Washington, DC

**An Arrangement in Flesh Color and Brown
(Arthur Jerome Eddy)** 1894
Oil on canvas, 82½ x 36½ in.
Arthur Jerome Eddy Memorial Collection, 1931.501.
The Art Institute of Chicago, IL

Stephane Mallarme 1894
Lithograph on paper, 3¹³⁄₁₆ x 2¾ in.
Freer Gallery of Art, Smithsonian, Washington, DC

Rose et Vert, l'Iris: Portrait of Miss Kinsella 1893-1902
Oil on canvas, 75½ x 35½ in.
Terra Foundation for the Arts, Daniel J. Terra Collection, 1987.32
Photograph © 1996 Courtesy of Terra Museum of American Art. Chicago, IL

The Little Rose of Lyme Regis 1895
Oil on canvas, 20 x 12¼ in.
William Wilkins Warren Fund
Courtesy of Museum of Fine Arts, Boston, MA

The Blacksmith of Lyme Regis 1895
Oil on canvas, 20 x 12¼ in.
William Wilkins Warren Fund
Courtesy of Museum of Fine Arts, Boston, MA

Brown and Gold: Self-Portrait c. 1900
Oil on canvas, 24½ x 18¼ in.
National Gallery of Art, Washington, DC
Gift of Edith Stuyvesant Gerry

Portrait of Charles Lang Freer 1902
Oil on wood panel, 20⅜ x 12½ in.
Freer Gallery of Art, Smithsonian, Washington, DC

ACKNOWLEDGEMENTS

The publisher is grateful to the following institutions for permission to reproduce the pictures on the pages noted below:

Miriam and Ira D. Wallach Division of Art, Prints and Photographs, The New York Public Library, Astor, Lenox and Tilden Foundations:
S. P. Avery Collection – 1, 9, 32, 33, 37, 38, 53, 82
A. E. Gallatin Collection – 19, 24
Prints Collection – 21

The Tate Gallery, London: 2, 49, 58/9, 62, 64, 66, 67

© The Phillips Collection, Washington, DC: 114

© The Frick Collection, New York: 68, 94, 115

Toledo Museum of Art, Toledo, OH: 54

Isabella Stewart Gardner Museum, Boston, MA: 50/1, 100/1

Hillstead Museum, Farmington, CT: 4, 44/5,

Courtesy of The Art Institute of Chicago: 6, 119, 121

© Hunterian Art Gallery, University of Glasgow: 7(both), 16, 60, 63, 111, 117

© The Detroit Institute of Arts: 61, 72

The Taft Museum, Cincinnati, OH: 10, 34/5,

Cincinnati Art Museum, Bequest of Herbert Greer French: 11

Hugh Lane Municipal Gallery of Modern Art, Dublin: 12

Glasgow University Library: 13

Freer Gallery of Art, Smithsonian, Washington, DC: 14, 15(T), 22(B), 23, 27, 28, 29, 30, 31, 36, 39, 47, 48, 52, 55, 57, 69, 73, 74/5, 79, 83, 84, 85, 87, 88/9, 92/3, 97, 98, 99, 102, 103, 104/5, 106, 107, 108/9, 113, 116, 118, 120, 122, 127

Courtesy of Terra Museum of American Art, Chicago, IL: 123

The Walters Art Gallery, Baltimore, MD: 110

The Mead Art Museum, Amherst College, MA: 90/1

Musée du Louvre, Paris: 15(B)

Worcester Art Museum, Worcester, MA: 76

Philadelphia Museum of Art, PH: 70/1, 96

The Metropolitan Museum of Art: 17, 18, 77, 95

Harvard University Art Museums: 22(T), 56, 78, 86

© Board of Trustees, National Gallery of Art, Washington, DC
25 (Rosenwald Collection), 26 (Rosenwald Collection), 40/1 (John Hay Whitney Collection), 46 (Harris Whittemore Collection), 126 (Gift of Edith Stuyvesant Gerry)

Wadsworth Atheneum, Hartford, CT: 42/3

Glasgow Museums: Art Gallery & Museum, Kelvongrove, Scotland: 65

Courtesy of Museum of Fine Arts, Boston, MA 80/1, 112, 124, 125